Modern Humanism:
Living Without Religion

Alfred Hobson
Neil Jenkins

Modern Humanism:
Living Without Religion

by

Alfred Hobson
Neil Jenkins

Adelphi Press
4-6 Effie Road, London SW6 1TD

First published in 1989 by Dene Books
Second edition printed and bound in the UK
Published by Adelphi Press
ISBN 1 85654 111 8

FOREWORD TO THE FIRST EDITION

In 1976 Bob Griffin, the Secretary of the Tyneside Humanist Society wrote a short simple guide to modern Humanism. He named it 'Humanist Attitudes', a booklet of over 50 pages in the form of answers to questions – questions which had arisen in the course of many talks on Humanism.

Bob was a remarkable and versatile man. A dedicated school teacher, he was a skilled amateur actor and film maker. He conducted the Humanist funeral service in a beautiful and moving film 'Death of a Miner' which is now in the BBC archives. He was keenly interested in politics and was for some years Chairman of the Newcastle upon Tyne Education Committee. At the age of 65 he stood for Parliament and nearly won the seat for Labour.

He played a leading part in the formation of the Tyneside Humanist Society in the early 1950s and for many years arranged weekly meetings. The many lively discussions influences the content of 'Humanist Attitudes' which had a wide sale in the UK and reached several countries overseas. He died in 1983 at the age of 82, active to the last.

The present authors decided to re-issue 'Humanist Attitudes' and bring it more up-to-date by including much new thinking. We have consequently renamed in 'Modern Humanism'. The original format has been kept of giving a Humanist answer to basic questions. There are of course many more questions than the 20 answered here.

THE AUTHORS

Alfred Hobson M.Sc. (London) is a retired lecturer in Social Sciences (mainly Economics and Public Administration) from New College, Durham. For many years Chairman, and later Treasurer, of the Tyneside Humanist Group.

Neil Jenkins Ph.D (Cantab), D.Sc. (Manitoba) is the retired Professor of Oral Physiology from the University of Newcastle upon Tyne, where his main research was on the prevention of tooth decay. He is President of the Tyneside Humanist Group.

PREFACE TO THE SECOND EDITION

We would like to thank those readers of the first edition for their favourable comments and critical suggestions which have encourage us to embark on this second edition into which many of the suggestions have been incorporated. We have enlarged the original title (Modern Humanism) to make it a more informative mini-definition of Humanism.

Alfred Hobson
Neil Jenkins

CONTENTS

INTRODUCTORY SUMMARY

Question One
What is Humanism?

The origin of the word 'Humanism'
The word 'Humanism' refers to the thought of the Renaissance, the 'rebirth' of the classical knowledge of Greece and Rome that took place during the 14th to the 17th centuries. Before the Renaissance, European education was chiefly concerned with the study of the Christian religion and preparation for life after death. During the Renaissance, opinions changed and the most liberal education came to consist of the study of Greece and Rome. As this was more concerned with the problems facing human beings in their ordinary lives, involving law, geometry, astronomy and medicine, its followers came to be known as Humanists. Today, the term is used in a different sense and refers to those who reject the supernatural views of Christianity (and other theistic religions) and who concentrate on searching for a reasoned answer to the problems facing people during their life on earth. Humanism of this type is variously known as Non-theistic, Scientific, Evolutionary or Secular. Secular Humanism is the most widely used term today. The word 'secular' has several definitions but as a description of Humanism it means dealing with the problems of the present world and rejecting supernatural explanations. It was first used in this sense in 1851 by G.J. Holyoake, the English rationalist and one of the founders of the co-operative movement.

The Main Humanist Ideas
Secular Humanists may have very different views on many subjects, for example they may belong to different political parties but they are in broad agreement on the following:-

a)   They do not think in terms of a God who created the universe, who controls our lives and who answers prayers (one reason for the name Humanism).

b) They think that moral ideas arose in the course of evolution rather than being of divine origin. The Humanist basis for morals is that nothing is more important than people. Humanists are concerned with improving happiness and welfare of the whole human race and think that improvement can be brought about by human effort alone, the second reason for the name Humanism.

c) They do not take their ideas about the origin and nature of the universe from sacred literature written many centuries ago. Humanists take their view from modern science whose theories are based on observation and experiment. They think that scientific method is the only way of adding to the stock of knowledge and discovering the relationship between events.

d) They see no convincing evidence for the existence of a life before birth or a life after death.

e) They continually examine and re-examine knowledge and ideas to consider ways and means of improving the world's environment and the human race as a species.

f) They try to keep their thinking up-to-date by heeding the following warning: Remember that you are human and sometimes make mistakes. Check your facts again and again. Be ready to go over old ground and to test again accepted ideas no matter what weight and authority there is behind them. Do not close your mind in the belief that you have reached the final truth or absolute certainty. New information is being added to the world's knowledge every day and some of it may compel you to change your ideas. Humanists are prepared to admit that they may be wrong.

While there is no Humanist Creed, Humanist organisations do draw up statements from time to time outlining their aims and attitudes to current problems. These are not fixed for all time and may change in the light of new knowledge or ideas. Statements can be obtained from:

British Humanist Association
47 Theobald's Road
London WC1X 8SP
Telephone: 0171-430 0908

International Humanist and Ethical Union
Niewe Gracht 69A
3512 LG, Utrecht
Netherlands

HUMANISM AND OTHER BELIEFS

Question Two
Is Humanism a Religion?

The answer to this question depends on how the word religion is defined. To most people in the western world, the idea of religion follows the dictionary definition of 'belief in a higher unseen controlling power and the morality connected therewith'. On this definition, Humanism is clearly not a religion as it rejects belief in the 'higher unseen controlling power'. Many Humanists are very clear that Humanism is not a religion and are unhappy about any attempts to stick the label 'religious' on them. The United Nations in their Charter of Human Rights suggest, on the other hand, that both theistic and non-theistic beliefs can be regarded as religions.

The main features of most of these types of belief are as follows:

1) **Theistic beliefs** are based on the existence of supernatural forces. Their followers accept the existence of a God (or gods and goddesses) whom they regard as the creator of the universe and who is considered to have the power over matter such as weather, crops, human behaviour and other natural phenomena. In many religions, the deity is a personal God who listens to and answers prayers. These religions are usually associated with a belief in an after-life with rewards and punishments. Traditional Christianity, Judaism and Islam are beliefs of this type.

2) **Non-theistic beliefs** are not based on the supernatural and usually consist of guide-lines for human behaviour which have been drawn up by one or more outstanding thinkers or teachers. Examples are:

a) **Confucianism.** Confucius (551–479 BC) lived through a chaotic time in China's history. He did not believe in a God or the soul. He became a teacher and drew up rules for good behaviour based on research into the customs of former times which he thought would provide the basis for a more stable society. His study of the way people behaved led him to formulate one version of the Golden Rule: Do not do to others what you would not like them to do to you.

b) **Buddhism**. Buddha (563 – 483 BC) drew up rules for behaviour based on practical knowledge and a strong belief in education. He too did not believe in a God or the soul but some of his followers introduced elements of the supernatural into Buddhism. One sect of modern Buddhism with over 11 million followers (mostly in Japan) describes itself as a Buddhist group with Humanist beliefs.

c) **Epicureanism**. Epicurus (342 – 270 BC) was born on the island of Samos in Ionia – an area noted for philosophers. When he was 18 a short stay in Athens aroused his interest in philosophy and, influenced by Democritus, he established a school of his own, settling in Athens in 307 BC. He taught that the prudent pursuit of pleasure was the main aim in life and that prudence was the real guide to happiness. A prudent person should reason about balancing pain and pleasure in the pursuit of happiness which was defined as 'tranquillity or quiet contentment.' His ideas quickly spread throughout Greece, Asia and Egypt and later they became a major philosophy in Rome – Hadrian, regarded by many as the greatest Roman Emperor, was a devoted Epicurean. Many of the Renaissance Humanists as well as the thinkers of the 18th century Enlightenment were Epicureans, e.g. Rousseau and Voltaire. Later, the ideas of Epicurus were misunderstood and the pursuit of happiness over-emphasised so that today an Epicurean is regarded by most people as a gourmet – one who delights in expensive foods and wines, rather than in 'quiet contentment'.

In England, a small group of influential people extended the Epicurean idea of personal pleasure to the promotion of general happiness. Their ideas came to be known by the name of Utilitarianism – the ethical principle of 'the greatest good for the greatest number.' The Utilitarians played a major part in 19th century legislation and worked for religious freedom, electoral reform, free trade, easier access to education, reform of the poor law and a reduction in harsh penalties for crime. Most of the leading Utilitarians were rationalists (that is, basing their lives on reason and not on divine revelation) and their leader Jeremy Bentham (1748 - 1832) was a confirmed atheist. Much of the legislation of the 20th century has been based on the utilitarian principle, which is also the inspiration of Humanist ethics.

d)   Other non-theistic beliefs include Stoicism, Rationalism, Positivism, Secularism, Free Thought, Agnosticism and Atheism.

Secular Humanism, like Confucianism and Buddhism, has a non-theistic set of beliefs. It has a philosophy of life and a framework of beliefs which provide a basis for a moral code so that it does serve the purpose of a religion. Does this give it the status of a religion? Some think it does. Sir Julian Huxley (1887 – 1975), grandson of T.H. Huxley, champion and defender of Darwin, thought that Humanism should be regarded as a non-theistic religion and expressed this view in his book 'Religion without Revelation,' published in 1927 and reprinted in 1967. However, because the term religion has for so long implied a belief in the supernatural, many Humanists think that Humanism should be described as a belief rather than as a religion. Other ways of describing Humanism include: Humanist stance, a stance for living, Humanist philosophy and the Humanist attitude.

In 1977 the Supreme Court of Alabama decided that Secular Humanism should have the status of a religion in that State. As the US Constitution forbids the teaching of religion in schools, this meant that Secular Humanism could not be taught in Alabama schools. Also, it was ordered that a number of textbooks should no longer be used as they were alleged to contain Humanist views.

The United Nations Declaration of Human Rights
In 1948 the General Assembly of the United Nations published the Universal Declaration of Human Rights in which Article 18

states that: 'Everyone has the right to freedom of thought, conscience and religion, this right includes freedom to change his religion or belief, and freedom either alone or in company with others and in public or private, to manifest his religion or belief, in teaching, practice, worship and observance'.

This declaration is not legally binding on member nations but they are expected to implement the recommendations. By 1976 the UN had agreed to strengthen and reaffirm the Universal Declaration in the form of two covenants – one on Economic, Social and Cultural Rights and one on Civil and Political Rights. Member nations ratifying these covenants would be legally bound to implement them. In the UK they were ratified on 20th May 1976.

In 1981 the UN agreed to the Declaration on the Elimination of all forms of Intolerance and Discrimination based on Religion or Belief. This declaration considerably extended and reinforced the content of Article 18 in the 1948 Universal Declaration of Human Rights.

In 1986 the UN expressed its serious concern that the 1981 Declaration was not being implemented and that there was far too much intolerance and discrimination about religion and belief. The UN therefore appointed a Special Rapporteur to examine the position and a full report was made to the UN in 1987. The report listed the many ways in which intolerance and discrimination was practised and recommended that members should take legal and administrative measures to eliminate them.

Question Three

Humanists tell me that thinking should be in terms of theories not beliefs. How then can it provide a foundation for a satisfying philosophy of life?

Humanism cannot provide absolutes and certainties for people who crave them. Humanists in serious conversation or writing try to avoid making untestable or unprovable dogmatic or doctrinaire statements. With our present state of knowledge, the universe is known to be so enormously complex that it cannot be fully understood. Those who demand certainties may condemn themselves to disappointment and unhappiness because no one can provide them with the beliefs they hope for.

Everybody will admit that even the most intelligent animals such as dogs and apes have no conception of many human ideas like politics, ethics or science. The human intellect has developed enormously during the several millions of years in which humanity has been evolving as a separate species. But we have no reason whatever to expect that it has developed sufficiently to enable us to understand fully the nature of the universe or why it exists. In spite of our great knowledge about the universe, including ideas about how it formed, the fact that it exists at all remains an inexplicable mystery. Humanists get used to the idea that the existence of the universe cannot be explained and prefer this to the acceptance of some untestable, mystical explanation such as creation by God. The realisation that there are no absolute certainties need not prevent us from enjoying thoroughly the many sources of happiness that the world can offer. Humanists in general are not puritanical or ascetic. They believe in enjoying to the full natural beauty, human companionship, food, drink, recreations and cultural pursuits always providing that their activities do not detract from the well-being of others.

SCIENTIFIC METHOD

Question Four
What is meant by 'scientific method' and why do Humanists attach so much importance to it?

Scientific method is the procedure followed by scientists to investigate the facts of their subject and how they are related to each other. Based on early writings, the procedure has usually been described as follows (but this description has been criticised, see page 14):

1) Observations (usually referred to as 'data') about a particular phenomenon are collected and checked for accuracy. Care is taken to ensure that the observations are sufficient in number and chosen randomly.
2) The observations are then studied to see if any regularities, patterns or generalisations can be found. This process is known as 'induction' – drawing general conclusions from individual observations.
3) Possible explanations ('hypotheses') are than devised that might account for the general conclusions, it being realised that some of the hypotheses will probably be wrong.
4) Controlled experiments are then conducted to attempt to decide which hypotheses are wrong and which might be right. In this procedure, two or more similar groups are chosen, one (the 'experimental' group) is subjected to whatever is being tested and the other group (the 'control' group) is not. Comparison of the two groups – which may be of inanimate objects, animals or people – can then decide whether the treatment has had any effect; if so, then the hypothesis is supported but further confirmatory experiments are required before it can be regarded as probably correct.

The procedure is well illustrated by considering experiments carried out in the 17th century to investigate the origin of the living things (maggots, flies, worms etc) that grow in stagnant water and heaps of decomposing organic matter. For centuries, following the teaching of Aristotle, it had been believed that these creatures developed by 'spontaneous generation' that is, without living parents (hypothesis 1). Some scientists suspected, however, that they could arise only from pre-existing living things (hypothesis 2). The two hypotheses were tested by the very simple experiment of taking two pieces of meat and covering one with several layers of cloth, leaving the other (the control) uncovered: both were allowed to stand in a warm environment for a few days. The result was that maggots were found on the uncovered (control) meat (from flies whose eggs had been laid there) but not on the covered meat from which, on hypotheses 1, they were supposed to be produced. This was the first indication that hypotheses 1 was incorrect and that spontaneous generation did not occur.

5) When experiments have suggested that a hypothesis is probably correct the next stage is to devise and carry out confirmatory experiments. On the assumption that the hypothesis is correct, predictions are made of the results of these experiments and if the predictions are fulfilled, then the hypothesis is made more probable though no amount of confirmatory evidence makes a hypothesis completely certain. The process of applying a theory or generalisation to individual cases is known as 'deduction'.

When a hypothesis is well established and covers a wide and important subject it is often referred to as a 'theory', such as the atomic theory or the theory of evolution. The terms 'hypothesis' and 'theory' are often loosely used interchangeably, however.

An example of confirming a hypothesis by testing a prediction of what should happen if it is true is provided by some experiments by Louis Pasteur. He finally disproved the idea of spontaneous generation by first showing that air contained many bacteria. When air was drawn through a tube containing a plug of cotton wool, living bacteria were retained on the plug. When a fluid containing substances that would readily putrefy was boiled to kill any bacteria it contained and then kept in a set of sealed tubes, no putrefaction occurred in any of them even after many months. When bacteria were introduced, either by letting in air or by putting in some of the cotton wool used as a plug, putrefaction occurred within a few days thus showing that living bacteria were necessary for putrefaction.

Pasteur predicted that air on the top of a high mountain, with its limited contact with living things, would contain fewer bacteria than air at ground level. He repeated the experiment with sealed tubes on the top of a high mountain and found that when the mountain air entered a set of twenty tubes containing putrefiable fluid, putrefaction occurred in only one of them. Evidently, the air that entered nineteen of the tubes contained no bacteria or too few to cause putrefaction within the duration of the experiment, thus confirming the hypothesis.

Deduction from well-established hypotheses is the basis of the solution of practical problems in applied science and technology. From the example just given, deduction from the hypothesis that putrefaction arises from bacteria in the air led to methods of food preservation and the prevention of infection in wounds.

The Reluctance of Scientists to Accept New Ideas
Pasteur's denial that spontaneous generation ever occurred was hotly contested by some of his fellow scientists. This is one of the many examples in the history of science showing that, contrary to the spirit of scientific method, scientists are sometimes reluctant to accept new ideas that contradict their previous pattern of thought. Even Einstein, one the greatest scientific geniuses of all time, never fully accepted the quantum theory.

Proof versus Falsification
Sir Karl Popper (1902–1994) one of the most distinguished of recent philosophers has emphasised that it is never possible to prove the validity of a hypothesis with absolute certainly. It may, however, be possible to disprove, or, to use Popper's term, to falsify it. As experiments or new facts falsify the incorrect hypotheses, they are rejected and those that remain may possibly be correct though in the light of further knowledge they too may be rejected or modified. Although Popper is logically

correct in stating that no amount of confirmatory evidence proves a hypothesis with certainty, such evidence is of great value because it makes the hypothesis more probable.

The Nature of Scientific Laws

In the early days of science, the conclusions induced from observations (stage 2 above) were thought to be based on divine commands as to how the universe worked. They were called 'laws' such as Newton's Law of Gravity and Kepler's Laws of Planetary Motion. This idea of the nature of scientific laws has caused great confusion of thought even to the present day. It must be emphasised that scientific laws are no more than conclusions arrived at from man-made observations. Like all scientific ideas, they are subject to change or rejection in the light of new evidence.

The Problem of Induction

The fact that scientific method is based on induction presents a problem, namely, that the validity of induction depends on certain assumptions such as the 'uniformity of nature' or 'uniformitarianism.' How do we know that this assumption is correct and that observations and conclusions made in one place at one time are valid in other places and other times? Only by making more observations and drawing conclusions by induction! Thus scientific method, based on induction, depends on the validity of assumptions that are themselves supported only by more induction. This presents a flaw in scientific method which is sometimes pointed out by theologians. The scientific answer is, of course, that the results obtained by scientific method have been applied to technology with outstanding success thus showing that, in practice, scientific method works.

Popper's Criticism of 'Classical' Scientific Method

Popper has suggested that, in practice, scientists do not usually follow the procedure outlined above. He thinks that it is not the collection of data that usually leads to the formulation of hypotheses but rather curiosity aroused by thinking about some well-established phenomenon or about data already collected by others. On Popper's view, the forming of the hypothesis is the first stage of scientific method followed by carrying out experiments or collecting data to falsify or support the hypothesis. The two procedures can be contrasted as follows. In 'classical' scientific method, a mass of data is collected and an attempt made to sort it out into a generalisation or law whose validity is then tested by experiment. Popper's approach would be: I wonder if X can be explained by Y or Z – let's carry out some experiments to find out! Popper believes that his procedure is not based on induction and hence avoids the logical flaw mentioned above. However, Popper does not seem to be entirely correct in his view because some scientific theories did arise from data that had already been collected before the theory was formulated and were, therefore, based on induction. One example is the theory of evolution, published in 1859 in the 'Origin of Species'. Darwin states in his autobiography: 'My first notebook was opened in 1837. I worked on truly Baconian principles and without any theory collected facts on a wholesale scale ... by printed enquiries, by conversation with skilful breeders and gardeners, and by extensive reading'.

The Origins of Scientific Method

The procedures of induction and deduction were first introduced by Aristotle (384 – 322 B.C.). However, Confucius (551 – 479 BC, see page 5) is reputed to have taught that 'Learning undigested by thought is labour lost; thought unassisted by learning is perilous'. This is a good summary of the ideas underlying scientific method made some 150 years before Aristotle though he would not be aware of it because in the West little was known about China until the 13th century. Aristotle's ideas were modified by a number of mediaeval thinkers among whom the 13th century Franciscan monk Roger Bacon introduced the idea of experiment, as opposed to speculation and argument, as the main source of knowledge. His namesake, Francis Bacon (1561 – 1626) is often regarded as the 'father' of scientific method. Although he did no scientific work himself he had great literary skills and his book Novum Organum (1620) made a great impact. In it he emphasised the importance of not jumping to conclusions too quickly and of avoiding prejudice (Aristotle had been prone to both these errors). He also pointed out the importance of experiments and the value of science in producing new inventions and a mastery over nature.

The Contrasting Skills of the Scientist

It is not always realised that scientific research involves two contrasting skills. In collecting data or recording the results of experiments great accuracy and the absence of bias or prejudice are necessary. The scientist must record what he sees not what he would like to see and much of this work can be a dull routine. In formulating hypotheses, on the other hand, a lively imaginative mind is required that is prepared to consider ideas from any source. In addition to disciplined thinking, useful ideas can come from hearsay, hunch and even dreams (at least one scientist has reported that the basis of an important idea came to him in a dream). But, having received ideas from whatever source, they must be subjected to strict experimental tests. The outstanding scientific geniuses are those with lively, inventive minds who can picture familiar things in a completely new light. Because few scientists excel in both making meticulous observation and in forming imaginative hypotheses and because different types of expertise are often involved in modern research, most of it is now done by groups of scientists working as a team.

Bias and How it is Avoided

Although ideally scientists should rid their minds of any bias or prejudice while carrying out experiments, in practice, there is nearly always some reason for hoping for a particular result, even if this is only subconscious.

Scientists who are testing their own hypotheses naturally hope that they are correct and that their experiment will support them and they may have an even stronger hope for a negative result if they are testing the hypothesis of a rival scientist! Also a great deal of research is carried out in industry where the hope is that a particular product will be effective or is superior to that of another firm.

Modern research methods using automatic recording instruments and statistical analysis minimise the risk that bias will affect the results but deciding what the result really means provides an opportunity for the wishes and hopes of the researcher to influence judgement. Good scientists are fully aware of this tendency and take precautions to avoid bias by carrying out, as far as is possible, what are called 'blind' experiments. In this procedure, the scientist who is comparing the experimental and control results does not know which is which. Suppose, for example, the effect of a fertiliser on plant growth is being tested. The scientist who measures the growth of the plants receiving the fertiliser (the experimental group) and those that were not (the control group) would not be told which group each plant belonged to until the measurements had been completed.

Although bias can be largely avoided or allowed for, there are on record a few scandals of dishonest scientists who deliberately misreported their results.

Why Humanists Attach so much Importance to Scientific Method

Humanists regard scientific method as important because it is now recognised as the only valid means of investigating factual questions and replaces the traditional sources of authority like Aristotle (regarded for centuries as an infallible source of knowledge) or divine revelation as recorded in sacred writings. Owing to the uncertainties of scientific observations and of the conclusions drawn from them, scientific knowledge is never final or complete and should be regarded as nothing more than the most probable conclusion from the available data.

It must be emphasised that the realm of scientific method is confined to facts and if, for any reason, scientific method cannot be applied to a factual question, such as the existence of God, then that question must be left open. Scientists should always be prepared to admit that they don't know the answer to a question if the evidence does not suggest one. However, a great deal of everyday life is concerned, not with facts, but with 'values' such as happiness, beauty or moral rectitude and here the application of science is very limited. Scientific method cannot provide decisions on values; there is no scientific way of deciding whether one object is more beautiful than another or whether one type of behaviour is more morally correct than another. Science can, however, investigate factual questions about value judgements, e.g. opinion polls can find out whether education has any effect on ideas about, say, abortion or whether income level makes any difference to such things as taste in music.

THE BEGINNING AND THE END OF THE WORLD

Question Five
How do Humanists account for the beginning of the world and how do they think it will end?

During the history of the human race, most thinkers seem to have formed ideas about how the world began, how it will end and what will happen to the people then living. Originally these ideas seem to have been in the forms of stories. Perhaps they were made up and told out of a natural delight in story telling. Many people like to have an explanation of some sort for everything, even if, in the pre-scientific age, it was little more than a folk tale or a fairy story. It is possible that what were originally told purely as stories for enjoyment became through years of retelling fossilised into religious beliefs.

Today, we can see that story telling about how the world began was bound to fail. The traditional attitude was that in the beginning an all-powerful God created the universe and the world out of nothing. The Humanist argues that the hypothesis of a creator God may have been useful in the past but today leads to more problems than it solves. In particular, if an all-powerful God created the universe, what brought about the existence of the all-powerful God in the first place?

Humanists accept the scientific view of the origin and end of the world of which the following is a very brief account. Over the last hundred years, astronomers using very much improved telescopes (optical, radio and those on satellites) have been able to find out a great deal about the size and nature of the universe and work out hypotheses about its origin and development. The question of the mechanism of the creation of the universe was, until the 1980s, regarded as beyond the scope of science and even beyond all human understanding. If creation is thought about as a common-sense problem there would seem to be only two ways in which it might be solved and both of these seem impossible! It might be thought (a) that the matter of the universe has always existed and Stephen Hawking in his best-seller 'A Brief History of Time' implies this in his proposal that space-time, like the earth's surface, has 'no boundary or edge.' However, the mind of non-mathematicians cannot picture this possibility. It is equally difficult to imagine the alternative (b) that matter was created out of nothing at one moment in time. However, it must be assumed that one of these ideas is true, in spite of the difficulties.

Most scientists now think that the second view is the more probable - that matter was created about 15 thousand million years ago in what is usually called the Big Bang. This is the idea that matter came into being as an extremely small mass that expanded with explosive violence projecting matter in all directions. This is often depicted as the outward movement of matter through space but is more accurately thought of as the expansion of space itself carrying matter with it. It is thought that in the tiniest fraction of a second after the Big Bang, the newly-created matter expanded from atomic size to about the size of a grapefruit (the inflation hypothesis) after which the expansion slowed down but still continues at the present time. Evidence for the expansion is based on the analysis by the spectroscope of the light from the distant galaxies. This shows what is called a 'redshift' which is usually interpreted as meaning that the galaxies are moving away from the earth and from each other (but the earth is not, of course, a central point from which the galaxies are moving). This means that the Universe is expanding at a rate that can be calculated from the size of the redshift and, by working backwards, it is possible to estimate approximately when the expansion began. The answer that emerges is between 10 and 20 thousand million years ago. It cannot be estimated more accurately than this because of uncertainties in measuring the redshift of the very distant galaxies.

The Big Bang should still only be regarded as a hypothesis although there are several lines of evidence for it and it is widely accepted. However, a few scientists have cast doubt on the main evidence (the apparent expansion of the universe) by suggesting that the redshift might conceivably be caused by something other than the recession of the galaxies.

When the Big Bang was first suggested in the 1950s no one understood how matter/energy* could be created out of nothing. Early in the 1980s, however, the idea was mooted that creation might have occurred by a process known as 'quantum fluctuation'. There is no space here to describe this complicated and abstruse process but it is explained by Paul Davies in his book 'God and the New Physics'. The proponents of this hypothesis think that quantum fluctuations could create matter/energy out of nothing: this may sound like a miracle but is not regarded as impossible on the basis of the quantum theory and does not require the intervention of anything resembling a creator God. Other scientists think that this overstates the case and that the universe must have contained 'something to fluctuate' (the origin of which cannot be explained) before the Big Bang occurred. Obviously, these speculations, on the very boundaries of knowledge and thought, must be regarded as tentative but future work may be expected to clarify them. Why the Big Bang occurred and why anything exists at all remain inexplicable.

The Results of the Big Bang

After its rapid inflation phase, the Big Bang is thought to have resulted in the formation of a vast swirling mass of hydrogen and helium. For reasons not yet understood the swirling mass divided up into separate clouds of matter that formed the nebulae, which, in turn condensed into the myriads of stars (some probably surrounded by planets) now known as galaxies. Our galaxy (the Milky Way) has a disc shape and contains about 100,000 million stars and it rotates about its axis every 225 million years. Several hundreds of millions of other similar galaxies are known to exist throughout the universe. The sun is a typical medium-sized star situated about one third of the way between the outer edge of our galaxy and its centre. The stars appear fainter than the sun simply because they are millions of times further away from the earth than is the sun.

Stars do not last forever - they form, emit energy while evolving through various stages and eventually, it is believed, most will end up as cold 'dead' worlds. In about 5 thousand million years our sun will begin to burn out. As it does so, astronomers think, it will expand into a type of star known as a red giant followed

* (see page 24-25)

by a contraction into another type of star known as a white dwarf which, over millions of years, will cool down to a dark, inert body. During the red giant stage the earth will become too hot to support life and all living things will become extinct. The earth may even be engulfed in the expanding sun. As some stars go through the terminal stages of this cycle, others are being formed from gas and dust in the space between the stars.

Fortunately, the time scale of these changes is so unimaginably vast that the final prospect of a dead earth need not be a matter of concern to us or interfere with our present happiness or enjoyment of life.

Question Six
If Humanism is not based on belief in God what is it based on?

With the development of science, especially in the 20th century, the idea of a God as a superhuman being living somewhere in outer space has become increasingly difficult to sustain. Consequently, for many years, Christians have been searching for a more realistic and up-to-date definition of God. It is not surprising therefore that as there are many Christian Sects, there are many different definitions of God. The Church of England in 1987 accepted that its members could now hold a variety of views on Christian beliefs.

Paul Tillich (1886 – 1965) was a German theologian who left Germany in 1933 to settle in the USA. He rejected the idea of a personal, all-knowing and all-powerful God with a super-human brain as something that was too abstract. Instead, he defined God as the 'ground of our being' which has led to much debate among Christians. This question might therefore be reworded: What do humanists think is the 'ground of our being'? In answer they would turn to the scientist.

Before discussing this, a short digression on the structure of matter may be helpful.

The Structure of Matter
The building blocks from which all the matter in the universe is made consist of 90 naturally occurring substances (and some additional man-made ones) called elements. An element is a substance that cannot be split into simpler substances by ordinary chemical methods (but see later). The elements are made up of particles called atoms, with a typical diameter of one hundred millionth of a centimetre, defined as the smallest particle of an element with the properties of that element. The weights of the atoms of each element (the 'atomic weight') are all different and are compared taking the weight of the atom of

oxygen to be 16. The atomic weights of the elements range from 1.008 for the simplest element (hydrogen) to 238 for the most complicated of natural elements (uranium). If the atom of an element is split up (as occurs in nuclear reactors and in natural radio-activity) the resulting pieces become atoms of a different element. For example, atoms of the radio-active element radium (atomic weight 226) break up spontaneously through many stages into helium (atomic weight 4) and lead (atomic weight 206).

When two or more atoms unite, they form a molecule and if the atoms are of different elements they form a compound. For example, two atoms of oxygen bound together form a molecule of oxygen and two atoms of hydrogen bound to one of oxygen form a molecule of the compound – water.

Chemistry and its Subdivisions
The study of the elements and their compounds (chemistry) is divided into:

1) Inorganic chemistry – the study of all the elements and their compounds except those of carbon.
2) Organic chemistry – the study of carbon compounds.

In the early days of chemistry, it was thought that substances that came from plants and animals (almost all of which are com-pounds of carbon) could only be obtained from living things and they were called organic compounds and the study of them therefore became known as organic chemistry. Later, it was discovered that some organic compounds could be made in the laboratory so the term organic chemistry now refers to the study of compounds of carbon whether they are normally produced by living things or not: the term organic chemistry is therefore rather misleading.

3) Biochemistry is the study of the composition of living things and of the chemical changes (metabolism) con-cerned with the processes of life.

Matter and Energy are Interconvertible
Physicists have shown that, in suitable circumstances, the mat-

ter that makes up the universe can be changed into energy and vice versa. Thus, the fundamental basis of the universe (the 'ground of our being') may be referred to as matter/energy. The following shows one way in which this conversion may happen and is the cause of the immense energy of the hydrogen bomb as well as being one of the sources of heat in the sun and other stars. When hydrogen atoms (atomic weight 1.008) are forced together at extremely high temperatures, each group of four atoms bind together to become one helium atom which weighs slightly less (4.003) than the four hydrogen atoms (4x1.008 = 4.032). The 0.7% of the weight of the hydrogen atoms not required to form the helium atoms is converted into very large quantities of energy. The energy released from 1 gram of hydrogen when it is converted into helium is three million times greater than that released when 1 gram of coal is burned.

Implications of the Importance of Matter/Energy

Thus, the Secular Humanist is a materialist in the philosophical sense, that is, believes that matter/energy is primary and, while in no way denying the importance of mind, intellect and emotion, believes that they arise from matter/energy and have no separate existence. This is known as monism - mind and body cannot be separated - and contrasts with the Christian belief in dualism, the view that mind and soul are different entities that can exist separately from the body. Although Humanists are philosophical materialists they are not usually materialists in the everyday sense of individuals whose main interests are in pursuing money and material things.

THE ORIGIN OF LIFE

Question Seven
How do Humanists explain the origin of life?

Humanists base their thinking on the scientist's hypotheses of how life arose and how living things evolved.

The Structure of Living Things
Biochemists have shown that the cells that make up the bodies of living things, including human beings, are made up of atoms and molecules of the same kind as make up the rest of the universe. Most cells contain about 70% of water and consist of a nucleus surrounded by the 'cytoplasm' – a very complex mixture of salts, several thousand different types of proteins and many other substances dissolved in water. Proteins are large molecules made up of hundreds, or even thousands, of molecules of about twenty different substances called amino acids linked together like a chain and, along with water, make up most of the weight of cells. Cells are surrounded by a membrane made up of two layers of fatty substances and some protein: it holds the cell together and lets food in and waste products out.

Within the nucleus are the chromosomes (in human cells, 46 in number) consisting of very long molecules of deoxy ribonucleic acid (DNA) arranged in a double helix, rather like two spiral staircases twisted around each other. DNA is the substance that makes up the genes. The 46 chromosomes differ considerably in size and therefore contain different numbers of genes. It is estimated that human cells contain about 100,000 genes. The DNA exerts its influence by controlling the formation of proteins; it decides which amino acids enter each protein and the order in which they are linked. The nature and amount of each protein formed determines an individual's characteristics such as the colour of the hair and the shape of the nose. DNA has the important property of forming copies of itself ('replicating') whenever a cell divides during growth; each copy enters and passes on its genetic information to the new cell formed from the division.

Cells vary greatly in size, shape and specialised function in different tissues such as bone cells, blood cells, nerve cells, but the size of most human cells range between 0.01 and 0.03mm in diameter. There are many species of animals that consist of one cell only. These are known as the protozoa and the amoeba is often taken as a typical example. Most animals contain a very large number of cells - an adult human body is thought to contain several hundred million million cells.

How Did Life Arise from Non-living Material?

The question of how cells evolved from non-living matter has not been definitely answered although possible mechanisms have been suggested and gained some experimental support. The following is a brief description of how it might have happened. Some simple organic substances (i.e. compounds of carbon) such as carbon monoxide, formaldehyde and cyanide and the nitrogen-containing compound ammonia, are known to be present in the stars and in space. These simple substances must therefore be formed quite readily in the absence of living things. It has been shown in experiments that if electric sparks are passed through mixtures of water, methane and ammonia for several days, amino acids (the building blocks of proteins) are formed. It is quite likely that, billions of years ago, the hot steamy shallow seas (what was called, at first rather jokingly, the 'primeval soup') and the atmosphere above it contained these simple substances and that lightning flashes and ultraviolet light from the sun provided sufficient energy to produce amino acids - the first step towards the formation of proteins. The substances that make up DNA were also probably formed at the same time and in the same way. The next step – the building up of proteins from the amino acids – is more difficult to envisage. In living cells, most of the chemical activities such as forming proteins, other cell constituents and releasing energy from fats and sugars, are carried out by the action of substances, themselves proteins, called enzymes. Proteins are formed by joining amino acids together by enzymes interacting in a most complicated way with DNA. How could proteins form in the primeval soup in the absence of both enzymes and DNA? There is no certain answer but very short chains of amino acids – much shorter than those in living cells – have been shown to form when solutions resembling primeval soup are evaporated, as might happen on the shores of lakes and seas. It is not unreasonable to speculate that during the hundreds of millions of years that elapsed before life began that larger molecules of proteins were formed in the same way and by a process of natural selection those that were most stable and could most readily be converted into larger chains would survive. Eventually, some of the early proteins probably acquired the special structures that enable them to act as enzymes after which protein formation would be greatly facilitated. It must be admitted, however, the formation of 'full size' proteins has not been reproduced in the laboratory from non-living matter.

The next stage would be the surrounding of the DNA-protein complex with a membrane to form something resembling a primitive cell. This process is not too difficult to imagine once fatty substances have been evolved as these fatty substances tend to form globules, not unlike the walls surrounding cells, quite spontaneously. It would be expected that some of the globules would entrap DNA and the other substances concerned with forming proteins. This could lead to the earliest single celled organisms from which, it is believed, were evolved (during more than 3,000 million years) the millions of species of plants and animals that live or have lived on earth.

THE EVOLUTION OF LIVING THINGS

Question Eight
How do Humanists think that plants, animals and people came into being?

Although the evidence is overwhelming that evolution has occurred from the simplest living things to produce the millions of species of higher plants and animals, the mechanism by which it took place is less certain. There is, however, general agreement among scientists that Darwin's theory of natural selection, or the 'survival of the fittest', is the main process by which plants and animals have evolved. It must be pointed out that fitness in the evolutionary sense has the specialised meaning of 'fitness to have offspring.' Evolution is not necessarily affected by fitness in the ordinary sense: people good at physical jerks or animals that run faster than usual do not influence evolution unless their achievements enable them to live longer and rear offspring more successfully.

Natural Selection in Evolution
Most species are very prolific in reproducing themselves, giving rise to far more offspring than can possible survive. Survival can be influenced in two main ways. The first that is believed to have played a part in evolution is change in the environment, such as climate or availability of food. Following such a change some species, or members of a species, will possess inherited characteristics that make them able to adjust to the change better than others and thus they will survive and reproduce at the expense of the less able. For example, it was found that when industrialisation advanced over the last century, light-coloured trees and walls became darker from deposits of soot or because lichens were killed by the pollution. In such areas inhabited by light and dark coloured moths, the proportion of dark moths gradually increased, because, compared with the light moths, they were less able to be seen and eaten by predators and thus would survive and produce more offspring. In this case, a natural genetic variation influenced survival following a change in the environment.

31

The Role of Mutations

The second factor influencing natural selection is the occurrence of what are called mutations. These are random changes which sometimes occur in genes (i.e. the DNA) of an individual living organism that produces a new characteristic not present in its parents but one that can be passed on to its offspring and to future generations. Although most mutations tend to be disadvantageous, some do make an individual better able to survive in the struggle for existence and to produce more offspring. An example is the mutation that occurred in mosquitoes that enabled them to resist insecticides, including the one known as DDT. When DDT was used on a large scale in an attempt to eliminate the insect-borne disease malaria, a mutation occurred which made some mosquitoes resistant to it. Those mosquitoes survived long enough to reproduce and they, and their resistant offspring, took over completely from the non-resistant insects that were wiped out: consequently malaria is still with us. The accumulations of mutations over millions of years is believed to be one way in which evolution occurred. Darwin's theory, combined with modern knowledge of genetics, is now known as 'neoDarwinism' ('new' Darwinism).

The Evolution of Complex Organs

Many thinkers, including some scientists, have expressed doubts as to whether natural selection could explain the evolution of such complex structures as the higher animals. Darwin himself raised the question particularly in relation to the eye. The various tissues of the eye could not function properly in isolation: the transparent cornea at the front of the eye would be useless without the light-sensitive cells of the retina at the back of the eye which, in turn would be useless without nerves connecting it to the brain. It is inconceivable that all the necessary structures could arise from one mutation. However, two points make this easier to understand. First, it seems likely evolution of complicated structures like the eye occurred in several stages; some of these stages are still present in lowly creatures. A light-sensitive spot in a depression on the skin, such as still exists in leeches, might have developed first from a mutation. If the depression became larger and filled with jelly-like material (as the result of another mutation), as in some worms, it would act as a primitive lens and pigment added to the sensitive cells would introduce some colour vision. Thus it may be envisaged that these steps, each caused by a mutation and each being retained because they had survival value, could lead to the evolution of the eye as we know it. The second factor is that recent developments in biochemistry have established that DNA can be broken up, sometimes into quite large sections, which may be re-assembled in the cell nucleus in a different order. This leads to mutations and, when large sections are involved, to several mutations simultaneously.

It has been known for many years that the cells in the body (except the sex cells) contain all the genes necessary for producing a whole body so that in any one cell most genes do not exert their effect. For example, a skin cell contains genes capable of producing all the tissues of the body but only those responsible for skin are 'switched on', the rest are made inactive by other substances in the cell. This means that mutations may arise in two ways: by changes in the structure of the genes themselves and by changes in the extent to which they are switched on.

The Role of Chance in Evolution
A criticism often heard of the theory of natural selection is that people 'can't believe that the human body evolved by chance'. It is true that mutations occur by chance but they are passed on to future generations only if the individual with the mutation lives long enough to have offspring. If the mutation allows them to be 'fitter', that is, live longer and have more offspring than individuals without the mutations, then the mutation is more likely to become established. In this way, the effects of the mutation, unlike the mutation itself, are not a matter of chance but influence evolution only if they increase the ability of the individual to pass on the mutation to future generations.

One of the classical arguments for the existence of God is based on the appearance of a design in living things. No one with even the slightest knowledge of the panorama of nature can fail to be impressed by the way plants and animals fit into their environment. The lightweight build of birds, the stream-lined shape of fish, as well as points of detail such as the webbed feet of waterbirds and the sharp teeth of flesh-eating animals are only a very few examples of what has been interpreted as evidence of special design. The theory of evolution by natural selection puts this argument into reverse. As living things diversified, as a result of natural variations or mutations, unless their shape and mode of living fitted their environment they simply did not survive. The beautiful adaptations shown by plants and animals exist because any other species that failed to develop these adaptations could not compete and became extinct. Another aspect of the argument from design is discussed in Questions 17. In spite of the gaps in our knowledge, Humanists accept the scientific view that evolution by natural selection is the most likely hypothesis to explain how living things, including humankind, came into being. The possible influence of additional, largely unknown factors cannot be dismissed, however. Humanists also think that the idea of evolution can be applied to the development of human society and its moral principles (See Question 11).

Creationists (people who believe that the different species of living things were separately created and have not evolved since their creation) base their beliefs on the biblical account of creation. They do not accept the massive evidence for evolution and give undue emphasis to the gaps in our knowledge and to any facts (and there are some) that are difficult to explain in evolutionary terms.

MIND AND SOUL

Question Nine
Even if the theory of evolution can account for plants and animals can it account for the mind and soul? Are not these different from matter?

Although it is obvious that the human body is a material object made of atoms and molecules like everything else in the universe, many people still think that the material body is in some way dominated by non-material entities of the mind, the will and the soul – a belief known as dualism. The expression 'victory of mind over matter' is sometimes heard meaning that the mind is supreme in forcing the body to undertake some activity. The terms mind, will and soul are used rather indiscriminately to refer to these entities but the words mind and soul really refer to different ideas.

The Mind
The dominance of the human species over the earth has occurred because of the large size of the human brain (cerebrum), especially the outer layer, the 'cerebral cortex' which controls consciousness, intelligence and reasoning. The cortex is about 4mm thick, much thicker than in the lower animals, and is made larger in area by being folded. The cortex of a human adult contains many billions of cells and each cell has innumerable connections with other brain cells so that the number and complexity of the 'circuits' through which nerve impulses may pass is enormous. This immense complexity makes it possible for human beings to be conscious, that is, aware of their existence and of their surroundings (a process that is still completely unexplained). This complexity also enables information received through the senses to be stored in the memory and to be processed as imagination and original thought. These activities of the brain are called 'mind' but the use of this word should not imply that the mind has an existence independent of the body. It is obvious that the mind can affect the body. An enthusiasm for life can hasten recovery from illness and a

35

competitive spirit can raise the physical stamina. There is also a close correlation between the condition of the body and the activity of the mind making it difficult to believe that the mind has a separate existence from the body. As the body grows in childhood so does the mind; when the body is fatigued, diseased or under the influence of drugs the mind is often affected in a similar way. Finally, as the body degenerates in old age, so usually does the mind. These considerations suggest that when the body dies, the mind dies with it.

The Soul
In contrast to the mind, the idea of the soul is a religious concept for which there is no precise, agreed definition. It is usually taken to refer to an immaterial element which is the seat of the moral attributes of a person. Religious leaders have differed greatly in their teaching about the soul; some believe that the soul is in some way superior to the body while others believe that both are equal and work together in harmony. The Roman Catholic Church accepts that the human body evolved from the lower animals, as Darwin suggested, but thinks that only human beings have souls, given to them by God. All religious leaders agree that the soul survives death and some think it is immortal. The idea of reincarnation is discussed in question 19.

The extensive studies of psychology, neurology and psychiatry have produced no evidence for the existence of the soul and the idea is virtually ignored by scientists. Humanists share this sceptical view and regard the soul as a figment of the theological imagination.

THE HUMANIST BASIS FOR MORALS

Question Ten
How do Humanists decide what is morally right and what is wrong?

First, it is desirable to clarify the meaning of the words 'morals' and 'ethics'. The word morals (from the Latin) refers to a set of rules about right and wrong behaviour (sometimes incorrectly thought to refer only to sexual behaviour). Ethics (from the Greek) is a branch of philosophy concerned with a critical analysis of different views on the nature and basis of morality throughout the course of history. These two words are often loosely used interchangeably.

In those parts of the world where Judaism, Christianity and Islam have been dominant, the assumption has been that everything was determined by God who was thought to be all-powerful, all-good and all-wise. People had therefore a duty to learn the will of God and obey it. What helped a person to understand and obey the will of God was good. What hindered the understanding and obeying the will of God was bad. This has led to great conflicts because the will of God was (and still is) interpreted differently by different sects and even by different priests and other leaders within each sect.

The starting point for the Humanist approach to morals is the proposition that human well-being is to be preferred to human misery and that nothing is more important than people. The expression 'well-being' is more appropriate than 'happiness' as this is the same for everybody (the provision of adequate food, reasonable housing, good health and education for the full development of personality). Happiness, on the other hand, is a very personal thing: to some it is beer and bingo, to others Bach and Beethoven. The preference for well-being to misery is a value judgement and cannot therefore be proved right or wrong but is surely accepted by all reasonable people. The Humanist criterion for a good or bad action is the effect of that action on human well-being. Those actions that improve well-being or decrease human misery are good whereas those actions that reduce well-being and increase misery are bad. If an action has no effect on human well-being then it can be regarded as morally neutral and it does not matter whether it is undertaken or not.

Humanist morals can be considered to be based on the Utilitarian principle of the 'greatest good for the the greatest number'.

The Different Levels of Morality

Most humanists apply their moral outlook at several levels. The first is in their personal lives where they try to be cheerful, friendly and helpful to those with whom they come into daily contact. They try to avoid causing them annoyance or distress. When confronted with unkind or aggressive personalities, they try to be tolerant and conciliatory and be fair and reasonable in their dealing with them in the hope that their attitude will be reciprocated. This approach can be summarised as 'trying to be a good neighbour' and living by the Golden Rule which has been a guide to good conduct for 2500 years. In the form given by Confucius 'Do not do to others what you would not like them to do to you' the rule is negative and merely an instruction not to be hurtful to people. The Jewish form 'Love thy neighbour as thyself' is more positive and the Christian form 'Do unto others as you would have them do to you' clearly suggests acts of kindliness and good neighbourliness on a reciprocal basis. Although in practice some moral principles of Christianity and Humanism are very similar the reasons for adopting them are very different. Christians try to follow the rule because it is God's will, as taught by Christ. Humanists adopt the rule because it is built into their conscience, they think it is a product of evolution (see Question 11), and furthers their aim of raising the level of human well-being. In addition to friendly personal contacts, many Humanists feel the urge to act in a wider field. This can be achieved by joining and working for charitable bodies, pressure groups and political parties in one's own community.

The Global Village

Humanists also think that, in these days of rapid transport and with television coverage of world events in almost every home, the whole world has to be regarded as a neighbour. Actions taken in one area can influence people far away, for example, high interest rates in a rich western country may prevent a poor third world country from borrowing to provide much needed development. Humanists feel impelled to support anti-racist movements and to help to build up an internationally-minded public opinion. This can be done by writing letters to the press or to MPs and, in some cases, writing articles or books, giving talks or raising funds. There is no shortage of ways to help. Humanists are encouraged to take an interest in world affairs as this puts them in a better position to decide which movement or charities are likely to be most effective in improving the well-being of the whole human race.

How can Humanists be sure about the effects of their actions?

A problem that greatly concerns Humanists is: How do they decide the effects of their actions and how can they be sure that what they think improves well-being does in fact do so? For example, should a street of well-kept houses be demolished to make way for a motorway that will reduce accidents and traffic jams? In a democracy, a finely balanced question like this can be investigated by public enquiries and local attitudes can be judged by conducting opinion polls. Admittedly, enquiries are often prejudiced and public opinion is often emotional and ill-informed but enquiries do help the process of discussion and debate. These procedures can be expected to become more effective with improved education and as more experience is gained. A decision can then be taken in accordance with majority opinion with generous compensation for the minority who are compelled to make sacrifices.

Another example of the difficulty in applying the Utilitarian principle of increasing the general level of human well-being is as follows. Is it wrong for poverty-stricken parents to steal food from a supermarket to feed their hungry children? The increased well-being from feeding the children is greater than the negligible effect of the loss by the supermarket. However, this act breaks the rule – upon which the smooth running of society depends – that stealing is wrong. Most Humanists believe in obeying the law unconditionally (although some might think it justifiable to break minor laws if this publicised or promoted some larger issue) and would therefore disapprove of this act. They would use their energy and whatever influence they have to help build a society in which there was no poverty. This, however, is a long term solution; in the short term, Humanists would consider this a case of extenuating circumstances and would probably favour a lenient punishment.

When it comes to wider issues of conflict between nations the morally fair solution is more difficult. Traditionally, nations have settled conflicts by war. Although the United Nations constitutes, for the first time in history, a body supported by almost every country in the world and although able to discuss disputes and suggest solutions, it is not strong enough to enforce its advice. Hence Humanists have a clear aim to work for the spreading of democracy and human rights and the strengthening of the United Nations to increase its authority.

The Working Compromise
In many situations, even after exhaustive analysis and discussion, the parties to a dispute cannot agree on a definite conclusion. In cases like this, that may occur at the personal, national and international level, Humanists advocate the principle of agreeing to a 'working compromise': an agreement to differ on some issues but still allowing a working relationship. The compromise may often be temporary and if it breaks down another compromise will have to be negotiated and this may lead to a more permanent solution.

The Fallibility of all Ethical Systems
It must be admitted that Humanists sometimes do have difficulty in deciding what action is likely to be most successful in raising the quality of human life. However, the adherents of theistic religions have similar difficulties as they are rarely able to agree what is the will of God and how it should be implemented. A study of the many ethical systems proposed over the centuries

shows that none of them is free from criticism and difficulties. Humanists think that their view point of morality - the effect of a decision on human well-being is sensible, easier to understand and no more difficult to apply than other moral criteria.

In spite of differences in outlook, the Humanist movement is, of course, willing to co-operate with Christians and the supporters of other religions and beliefs in the search for, and the implementation of, agreed policies and activities for promoting human well-being.

While the welfare of human beings is the main concern of Humanists, it is realised that this should not be at the expense of animals. The higher animals can feel pain and show clear signs of suffering emotional stress. Animals have been (and still are) subjected to appalling cruelty as sources of food, in performing work, as sporting objects and even as pets. Without being sentimental or unreasonable, many Humanists would include the welfare of animals in their moral code.

THE ORIGIN OF MORALS

Question Eleven
How do Humanists account for the origin of morals? Have not morals arisen from religious belief?

Today there are many people who never go to church and either do not believe in God at all or have only a vague notion of a God but do not think that He has any influence over their everyday lives. However, they are law-abiding citizens who get on well with their neighbours and play a responsible part in the community. From a moral point of view they cannot be distinguished from devoutly religious people. Thus moral behaviour does not depend on having a religious faith although many people do not seem to realise that there can be a basis for morals other than religion. A further illustration of the independence of morals from religion is that many books that deal with ethics in great depth (and often at excessive length!) either make no mention at all of Christianity or other religions, or mention them only incidentally. If morals do not arise from religion, where do they come from?

Evolutionary Hypotheses of the Origins of Morals
The Humanist thinks that morals are a product of evolution although the details of how this might have occurred are still controversial.

The study of heredity has shown that many physical characteristics of individuals, such as hair colour, height and body shape are inherited that is, dependent on the structure of the DNA derived from both parents. It would be expected that some aspects of personality are also inherited. However, it is also clear that environment may have a great influence on development. A child with genes for tallness may not achieve full potential if it is grossly undernourished and lives in a disease-ridden environment.

Group Selection

There is no doubt that altruism – the taking of risks or making of sacrifices for the benefit of others – exists among animals other than humankind. When predators are seen, alarm calls are often made by birds and mammals who draw attention to themselves (thereby increasing the risk of being caught) but give a warning enabling other members of the group to take evasive action. This suggests that moral behaviour has a biological, rather than a divine, origin.

Darwin pointed out that, in the early social life of humankind, several individuals working together could undertake larger projects and acquire greater safety from the many hazards that confronted them than if they acted separately. For example, a group of hunters could catch more and larger animals for food and defend their homes more effectively against dangers such as floods or predators than could individuals acting singly. It seems reasonable to suppose that in the course of evolution people possessing genes that favour co-operation with others, and have altruistic ideas of living with the interests of others in mind, tend to have a better chance of survival. Thus, the argument runs, altruistic people will live longer and have the opportunity to have larger families. In this way, it is suggested, the urge to co-operate became built into the human personality.

Environmental factors would also tend to reinforce the effects of genes on altruism. Children brought up in an altruistic family would tend to regard friendly co-operation as the accepted pattern of behaviour (an example of the spread of what Dawkins has called 'memes', see page 75). (On the other hand children often oppose the views of their parents, especially in a rapidly developing society in which succeeding generations have widely differing opinions).

This idea, that altruism developed because co-operative people survive better, is called 'group selection' and, although quite widely accepted, has been criticised on three main grounds. First, some evolutionists think that natural selection works only on individuals and not on groups. However, it might be expected that a mutation for altruism in an individual would, after several generations, lead to the birth of a sufficient number of people with the mutation for them to influence the group. In addition, the example set by those with the mutation would be expected to have some effect on the behaviour of the group, as mentioned above. Secondly, doubt has been expressed as to whether altruism is an inherited trait although, even if it is not, the example of altruistic parents would be expected to influence their children. The controversy between genetic and environmental effects (nature versus nurture) is still unsettled but it is reasonable to suppose that both are important and that they interact with each other. The third criticism of group selection is that sometimes selfish people, especially in an acquisitive society, become rich, influential and may even dominate the group. If it is assumed that altruism is inherited, then presumably selfishness is also inherited. This raises the question as to whether selfish people would eventually outnumber the altruistic members of society – the opposite of what the group selection theory suggests. This can be answered by the observation that people acquire a mixture of selfish and altruistic traits in varying proportions (by both genetic and environmental factors) and this could explain the range of behaviour from the criminal to the saintly. In a mature society, an approximate equilibrium is eventually reached between these opposing groups – what some sociologists have called an 'evolutionary stable strategy'. The position of the equilibrium obviously varies in different societies and at different times. Sometimes a mafia-like criminal class or a ruthless dictator may be in control while, in a liberal democracy, the altruistic members may dominate and keep in check the selfish and criminal minority.

The Selfish Gene Hypothesis

Another hypothesis to explain the origin of morals is based on what the zoologist Richard Dawkins has rather confusingly called (in his influential book with the same name) the 'selfish gene'. This does not mean a gene that makes an individual selfish in the ordinary sense, but one that makes people act in such a way as to favour the survival of their own genes some of which are, of course, shared with relatives. The continuation of the human race depends on the willingness of parents to feed and care for their young and, to a lesser extent, for others with whom they have a close family relationship (kinship). In other words, they behave in such a way as to increase the chances of their children and relatives surviving and being in a position to pass on their genes to future generations. This idea was rather whimsically illustrated by a remark said to have been made in a pub by Professor J.B.S. Haldane (1892 – 1964) the distinguished biochemist, mathematician and geneticist. Asked whether he would be prepared to die to save a brother he replied: 'No, but I would for three brothers or nine cousins!' These two groups of relatives would be able to pass on more copies of his genes than would be lost if he had died (brothers share half of a individual's genes and cousins one eighth).

Kin Selection and Reciprocal Altruism
Thus, it is suggested, altruism was originally limited to close family members but as societies evolved, it gradually extended to others. One suggested basis for the widening of altruism is that it occurred from reciprocating helpful acts. This is found even in animals who are often seen to help each other, for example, a pair of monkeys may take turns to groom each other. In an experiment to investigate the idea of 'reciprocal altruism' the cries for help from several monkeys were tape-recorded. When the calls were played back, the monkeys responded most vigorously to the calls from those monkeys that had previously groomed them.

On present knowledge, it is not yet possible to choose between these hypotheses that attempt to explain the development of altruism in the course of human evolution. The important point is that there are these several ideas that give plausible explanations for altruism and it is not necessary to assume that it arose from divine revelation or that it requires a belief in God.

The Present Day Evolution of Morals
The evolution of morals is continuing to this day. As the environment changes and knowledge increases so moral attitudes and the laws based on them change. This can lead to conflict in society. Attitudes to divorce, family planning, abortion, race and armaments are very different today from what they were a few decades ago although these changes are

not welcomed by all. Another example is the growing realisation that the earth's environment is a delicate ecological balance which requires world-wide co-operation for its protection for both present and future generations.

Why are Humanists Concerned about Others?

A further question that arises is why should a Humanist be concerned about the welfare of others especially when this involves a sacrifice of time, money or convenience? The Humanist answer is that, as mentioned above, some measure of altruism is built into all human personalities (it is well-known that there is even 'honour among thieves'). We assume that others, like ourselves, do not like to suffer pain and therefore it gives us pain to see others impoverished or hurt. In our dealings with others, it pays us to be fair, just and honest, hoping that they will be the same with us.

We have at present no power to modify genetic influences on behaviour. This may become possible in the future with advances in genetic engineering although it is doubtful whether it would ever be desirable. Society is based on the assumption that we have control over environmental factors that affect moral behaviour, such as education and parental example. Education and parental influence and the type of government can enhance altruism and discourage selfishness. Humanists can use their votes and personal influence to encourage those who are altruistic and restrain those who are selfish.

Some experiments have suggested that, among environmental factors, the provision of a dietary supplement of minerals and vitamins can raise the level of academic achievement and reduce disruptive behaviour. The result of these experiments are still in dispute but it seems unlikely that these supplements would benefit children on a varied, well-balance diet but might affect those receiving a diet deficient in these substances.

CONSCIENCE

Question Twelve
What is the Humanist attitude to conscience?

The traditional Christian belief about conscience is that it acted like a receiving apparatus, a sort of inner ear, for the reception of divinely inspired messages that gives guidance on moral problems. The Humanist rejects this view and thinks that conscience arises from living in a community and from being brought up to observe its laws and customs.

In any community there is a centre of authority. In a family with a young baby the parents make the decisions concerning the baby's welfare. From the first beginnings of awareness the baby realises that the parents are the source of comfort, food, warmth and cleanliness. The baby soon becomes aware that there are ways of behaving which the parents regard as good or bad. If the baby behaves well and pleases the parents it learns that it will be rewarded with cuddles, kisses and smiles. If it behaves badly it learns to expect disapproving words and gestures and possibly some form of punishment. The baby becomes a child and is made to feel pleased with itself if its behaviour meets with the approval of its parents. On the other hand if its behaviour is disapproved of the parents' reaction will give it a guilty feeling. There is therefore usually instilled into the child's mind (including the subconscious) a sense of the parents' attitude to right and wrong. This feeling of guilt or of self-satisfaction is what is meant by conscience.

As children grow up and they come into contact with a wider community they find that some customs have been given the force of law, the aim of which is to maintain a stable society. If the laws are not obeyed, society may exact a punishment, thus reinforcing and extending the sense of right and wrong.

However, people do not always observe the moral codes and may sometimes break the law. How can their conscience allow this to happen? There are three main reasons for this. First, temptations arising from greed, jealousy, selfishness or arrogance may be too great for conscience to control. Secondly, some people may never have been taught the difference between right and wrong or given a basis upon which they could make their own distinctions between right and wrong. Thirdly, many people regard some customs or laws as being out-of-date and therefore they suffer little in the way of a guilty conscience when they fail to observe them.

Ideally in a democracy all laws should be based on consent but sometimes laws are kept on the statute book long after most people have withdrawn their consent. Where there is a dictatorship, many people will regard laws as imposed to maintain a society which is deficient in human rights and fairness. Consequently they have a clear conscience in disobeying laws which they regard an undemocratic.

Changing Standards of Right and Wrong
Environmental, cultural and educational conditions change and this leads to change in customs and laws. Actions and attitudes which were once regarded as normal are today unacceptable or seriously questioned, e.g. slavery, child labour, colonial wars. The pendulum can also swing the other way. Actions viewed with displeasure in former years may become accepted. Thus divorce and contraception were accepted by only a few in the last century and abortion was illegal in Britain until quite recently. Today in a more liberal society these are widely accepted and, with the exception of abortion, cause few qualms of conscience.

Statistics show that crime and delinquency have risen greatly in recent years, especially amongst young people, implying that conscience has been 'turned down' to a lower level. Many reasons have been suggested for this:

a)   The tendency for punishments to be more lenient. This has led to a more relaxed society but at the cost of more fear and nervousness for many.

b) Lack of parental control in broken homes or in families with both parents working.
c) Poverty and boredom arising from unemployment along with advertisements encouraging high spending.
d) The decline in church and Sunday school attendance and consequent lack of religious and moral teaching.

Humanists would, of course, deny that religious instructions are necessary for teaching moral standards, even if they did fulfil this role in the past.

Humanists would wish to encourage more research into the causes of crime so that the relative importance of the above and any other factors can be assessed. The prevention of crime can be undertaken rationally only if there is more evidence about its causes. It is self-evident that the present methods of dealing with crime are largely ineffective.

A systematic comparison is needed of the numbers of offenders who become habitual criminals after receiving different penalties such as imprisonment, fining or community service. This research would give an indication of which methods acted as deterrents and which reformed and rehabilitated, rather than merely punished, offenders. It is obvious that such research is difficult and expensive and would involve the study of large numbers of offenders over many years but its importance would justify a major effort.

The Internationality of Conscience
While a change in morals is taking place there is inevitably a state of conflict in society. The scope of conflict has steadily widened. In early times conflicts would be within or between families. The formation of tribes and nations required new customs and laws as each group became larger. Today, we are realising more and more that nations are interdependent.

Groups of nations are linking together for common action, such as the European Community and the Organisation for African Unity. Customs and laws appropriate to the individual nation became inappropriate when the nation becomes a member of a group. Although it seems obvious, some nations and individual politicians do not appear to realise that the success of any international organisation depends on the willingness of each member to sacrifice some of its sovereignty for the benefit of the group.

Thus while the meaning of conscience remains the same (a feeling of satisfaction or guilt from obeying or disobeying customs and laws that protect the community) the scope of conscience has steadily widened. The human conscience now has to wrestle with questions affecting not only the welfare of groups of nations but the whole world.

SCIENCE AND RESPONSIBILITY

Question Thirteen

Humanism seems to put all its trust in science. What about pollution from pesticides and fertilisers and the harmful effects of additives in food? What about vehicle exhausts and factory smoke that causes acid rain? Scientists are responsible for the invention of chemical and nuclear weapons as well as for polluting the environment.

In this question two separate indictments are laid against scientists. The first refers to environmental pollution and the second is the suggestion that scientists are responsible for chemical and nuclear weapons.

Pesticides and Fertilisers

It is, of course, obvious that scientists were responsible for finding out experimentally which substances would act as pesticides and fertilisers and this was done in order to increase food production. Later, perhaps from the use of larger quantities than were really necessary, it began to be realised that potentially harmful residues of pesticides entered foods and that fertilisers (especially nitrates) seeped into some water supplies at undesirably high concentrations. This is now well-known and pressure of public opinion is forcing governments to restrict their use. Farmers, using information provided by scientists, were therefore inadvertently responsible for this pollution.

Food Additives

Food additives are used for a variety of reasons. Some (for example vitamins C and B1, and the minerals, calcium and iron) increase the nutritive value of the foods to which they are added. Other additives improve appearance, intensify flavour or lengthen the shelf-life. In other words, while some additives are beneficial to the consumer others are mainly for the profit of industry or the shopkeeper. Scientists in the food industry were responsible for suggesting which substances might be used and some additives have since been shown (by other scientists) to be possibly harmful, at least to some sensitive people. Whether the amounts used in food reach harmful levels is a very controversial question.

In most developed countries there are official bodies who monitor and control the permitted levels of additives on the advice of yet more scientists. Clearly, the responsibility is divided among several groups, of which scientists are only one and their contributions are mostly technical and advisory, rather than making decisions.

Industrial Pollution

Many industrial processes, whose end-products are of great benefit to society, do unfortunately involve the production of unpleasant and dangerous by-products which may enter the environment. Coal-burning power stations produce sulphur-containing smoke that helps to form acid rain, the petrol engines of cars pollute the atmosphere with carbon monoxide and lead; nuclear power stations form waste products that remain dangerously radio-active for many centuries.

Scientists have worked out methods of avoiding or dealing with most of these problems but their application is very expensive. It has to be realised that the price of many goods would rise markedly if manufacturers adopted the complicated precautions necessary to make industry pollution-free. Although much improvement has been made in recent years, largely in response to public demand, a more complete control of pollution requires the introduction and vigorous enforcement of legislation limiting or stopping the release of toxic wastes. Sadly, governments are reluctant to take this drastic action.

The alternatives to accepting the high cost of reducing pollution are a return to a more primitive technology (which is unlikely) or the development of new methods of manufacture and energy production that do not cause pollution. Windmills, solar panels and tidal power could be used to generate electricity but whether on a scale to meet modern energy requirements is uncertain. Their development would also be expensive and take many years to complete. Nuclear power prevents many forms of pollution but raises the equally serious and still unsolved problems of storing nuclear waste.

The effect of industry on the environment has been obvious for generations but was tolerated by the public and the industrialists who were directly responsible regarded it as a nuisance and inconvenience rather than a menace to health and well-being. Only in recent decades have the disastrous effects been fully realised of acid rain, water pollution and the release into the atmosphere of substances contributing to the 'greenhouse' effect. Some environmentalists (and they may not be entirely alarmist) warn that humankind and other species of living things may be on the way to extinction unless urgent steps are taken to put matters right. Fortunately, public opinion is now fully aware of the problem and pressure on governments and industry is beginning to show results. Again responsibility is divided. Industrialists, politicians, scientists and the general public all share the blame.

Nuclear and Chemical Weapons
The decision to develop and stock-pile nuclear and chemical weapons was a political one based on the belief that they preserve the international peace. It is the fear, real or imaginary, of potential aggression that leads to majority support for the defence policies involving these weapons. The scientists who invented nuclear weapons during the second world war realised that the survival of democracy depended on the production of an atomic weapon before the totalitarian powers produced one, although many scientists were aware of the horrendous implications of nuclear weapons and worked with an uneasy conscience. The decision after the war to produce the even more powerful hydrogen bomb was a political one aimed at deterring further aggression that was feared in the Cold War atmosphere at the time.

The use of chemical weapons has a long history: the ancient Greeks are said to have used sulphur fumes to poison and choke their enemies. 'Greek fire', a combustible mixture of uncertain composition, was used to set fire to enemy ships in the 7th century. Evidently military men exploited early scientific knowledge for use in weapons – a practice that has continued to the present day. However much it may be regretted (and Humanists regret it very strongly) it would seem that for as long as there is an armaments industry, some of the vast array of scientific knowledge will be applied to weaponry. Governments (including democratic governments and therefore the public), share the responsibility for this use of science in the name of defence.

The Role of Democracy

The decisions about how to apply scientific knowledge are made by politicians, industrialists and financiers. In a democracy there is an elaborate system by which many people vote to elect politicians. Thus, ultimately the voters are collectively responsible for what politicians do. Unfortunately, policies that involve the side effects of applied science are seldom election issues and political parties may have general programmes which gain the approval of the majority of voters but also carry out policies involving environmental damage. Politicians have to rely on information supplied by experts who may fail to point out (or even may not have foreseen) unpleasant side effects, especially if it is in the interests of employers to do so. Similarly, the voters may not be informed. Voters are informed by the media and if the media are ignorant or (worse) deliberately mislead them, voters will not be able to make a rational choice between alternative policies.

Humanists think that strengthening democratic institutions is the most effective way of encouraging a sense of responsibility and this must be accompanied by free access to information: too often, even in democracies, governments try to conceal information from the public. It may be objected that one citizen has little influence on public affairs but in a democracy there are many ways in which public opinion can make itself felt. Letters can be written to politicians and to the press, pressure groups can be formed which, if successful, have their message taken up by the media (this is the modern substitute for holding public meetings, a procedure that TV has made almost obsolete, except on a very small scale).

Conclusion

Thus when things go wrong in society it is unreasonable to pin the blame on to any one person or group, such as scientists. In a democracy, a large number of people and groups are responsible for mistakes or the unforeseen consequences of their actions.

SCIENCE AND RELIGION

Question Fourteen
Are science and religion compatible?

Secular Humanists think that science and theistic religions are not compatible because their approaches to basic beliefs are so different. The religious approach is based on faith and most religious beliefs such as the existence of God, heaven, hell and the validity of divine revelation are untestable by scientific method. Humanists fully realise that over the last century or so, theological ideas have changed, for example, the Darwinian theory of evolution has been accepted by most Christian sects and the Genesis story is now regarded as a myth. This has led to the very real difficulty of knowing what theologians do believe. It is a common experience for Humanists to explain why they do not accept some particular theological belief only to be told that some theologians have long since given up that belief themselves! Even if theologians, following the example of scientists, have dropped or modified many old concepts, the ideas they still do accept are based either on religious experience (that, however convincing to those that have them, are of no evidential value to others) or on faith or on modern interpretation of the validity of the scriptures.

Science relies on observed facts and experiments to support it. Its hypotheses and conclusions are always based on probability, never on certainty. Old ideas are amended or replaced in the light of new knowledge.

In spite of this conflict of approach between science and religion many scientists do adhere to Christianity or other theistic religion. How do they reconcile these two very different points of view? The following are among the most popular attempts to make this reconciliation although Humanists do not think any of them are successful:

1)   Some scientists have two 'watertight' compartments in their minds and make no attempt to fit together their religious and scientific views. Newton and Faraday were

two such scientists. This is understandable because when they lived, the two main scientific ideas that conflict with the Bible, that is, the evolution of life and the great age of the earth, had not been developed. It is difficult to understand how a scientist can hold this position today, although some do: when asked about this, a common reply is that religious beliefs are 'too personal a matter to discuss'.

2) A more rational attempt to reconcile religious and scientific views is often referred to as the 'God of the gaps'. This means that although science can explain many things a problem may eventually be reached which science cannot solve. Until very recently, science could offer no hypothesis to explain how matter/energy was created in the first place (one has now been proposed, see page 21). Certain steps in the evolution of complex living matter from non-living organic compounds cannot yet be fully explained (see page 28). If science cannot answer these questions then the intervention of God is suggested. However, as science progresses, the gaps are being filled.

Widespread scientific thinking is a very youthful activity (it is barely one hundred years old) and future scientists may provide more answers. At the same time, we must accept human limitation: there is no reason to expect that the human intellect will ever by able to answer all fundamental questions.

3) Some scientists, although not necessarily accepting all the beliefs of a particular religion, think that the human mind needs a 'something' more ethereal and mystical than the matter-of-fact approach of science. They find religious practices to be emotionally satisfying, fulfilling some indefinable need. A psychologist once said that, as the human mind could not think rationally all the time, he went to church every Sunday to get his weekly dose of irrationality! The Humanist also often feels the need for what some would regard as non-rational or 'unwinding' activities and they meet it by taking part in, for example, competitive games, walking in the country (even in uncomfortable conditions!), reading poetry or fiction, dancing or listening to pop music.

4) Another attempt to reconcile the two suggests that science and religion are about different things: science is about facts and religion is about values. There is some truth in this but Humanists would point out that Christians claim that their religion is based on the belief in the alleged historical facts of the birth, death and resurrection of Jesus Christ. Some of these beliefs are not only outside our experience but completely contrary to it: hence the scepticism of Humanists. Humanists think that they have a guide to moral values independently of divine revelation, namely, that we should consider how our actions affect the well-being of others. The suggested contrast between the content of religion (values) and science (facts) is not therefore clear-cut.

5) Other scientists explain modestly that a scientific training does not enable them to express opinions on religious matters any more than a theological training enables a person to express an opinion on science. So they assume that theologians 'know what they are talking about' and accept their views. Humanists would reply that scientists are entitled to express opinions on the factual statements that Christianity has traditionally accepted (there is doubt as to how many Christians accept them today). The probability, for example, of the virgin birth, the resurrection and the after-life is becoming less and less as our knowledge grows. Scientists are also entitled to point out the difference between belief based on scientific method and belief based on faith.

6) Another attempt to reconcile science and religion is to suggest that religious belief in the unseen is not qualitatively different from that of some of the beliefs of scientists. Theologians talk about the soul, divine revelation and eternal life whilst the scientists talk about electrons, neutrons and black holes. It must be admitted that some ideas emanating from the quantum theory are as much contrary to everyday experience as are many mystical religious beliefs. However, although the scientist deals with things that are unseen they are based either on experimental evidence or on deductions from this evidence and ideas about them change in the light of new

knowledge. Whilst theological ideas have changed (usually from the impact of science) some, such as belief in a personal God, are still based ultimately on faith. Scientists suggest tentative hypotheses and if experiments do not decide which hypothesis is correct, they accept that the answer is not at present known.

7) A modern view about God as a designer which some scientists support is based on what is called the 'anthropic principle'. This is a group of ideas defined in different ways by different authors (and described by one writer as a 'chaos of concepts'!). Many of the arguments are highly technical (for a popular account, see Cosmic Coincidences by John Gribbon and Martin Rees) but the one most readily understood points out that if the two opposing forces that operated during and after the Big Bang had not been so delicately balanced, the universe could not have developed in a way that permitted the formation of living things. The outward force of the Big Bang projecting the newly-formed matter in all directions as space expanded was opposed by the force of gravity that caused particles to attract each other and to cling together. If gravity had only been slightly more powerful (or the Big Bang slightly less powerful) then the particles would never have separated sufficiently to form the widely spaced galaxies that eventually produced stars, planets and (at least on our earth) living things. If gravity had been only slightly less powerful (or Big Bang more powerful) matter would have been forced apart too rapidly to coalesce into galaxies and would remain as an ever-expanding cloud of gas. The fact that these forces were 'just right' to allow both the dispersion of matter and its eventual collecting together as galaxies is taken as evidence of the existence of a designer, as the possibility that this balance could occur by chance is considered to be extremely remote. This is only one of several coincidences upon which the existence of life has depended.

Attempts to counter this as an argument for a creator have taken two forms. In one, the 'many worlds' hypothesis, it is suggested that many other universes exist, (or have existed in the past or will exist in the future), in which this balance does not occur. If there are many universes, then it is quite possible that one might have the right balance of forces by chance, and that is our universe. There is, of course, no evidence for the existence of these multiple universes and the idea is not regarded as likely or realistic and would not seem to be testable. The second way of avoiding the implications of the anthropic principle is based on the inflation theory (page 20) and suggests that during the minutest part of a second after the Big Bang the conditions of enormous temperature and pressure were such that the forces of nature that we know were not operative. It is speculated that the expansion was caused by an extremely powerful repulsive force which dispersed matter throughout the universe in a small fraction of a second and only after this inflation had occurred did gravity take over. It is suggested that changes occurring during the inflation led to a balance of forces which allowed the universe to develop into its present form.

Conclusion
So, because Humanists think these arguments are unconvincing, they consider science and religion to be fundamentally incompatible. It is fully realised that Christian theologians now make more use of scientific method in exploring some aspects of the historical basis of Christianity, for example, textual criticism of the Bible, archaeological studies of the Middle East and the rejection of the Genesis account of the world's origin. Consideration is also being given by theologians to the contents of the Dead Sea Scrolls - some 500 manuscripts relating to the period 250 BC to 70 AD found in 1947 in caves near the Dead Sea. Their full contents have not yet been released but are thought to shed new light on the origin of Christianity. Humanists welcome the application of science to religious problems, which is reducing the number of beliefs based on faith.

The Value of Religion
Humanists do not deny the value of religion to many people as a source of comfort, uplifting ideas and moral inspiration. Humanists, too, derive comfort and inspiration from their own views. Once they have adjusted to their conclusion that humankind cannot call on divine help but must work out its own

destiny, Humanists receive great uplift by reflecting on human scientific achievement and responding to the moral challenge of trying to raise the general level of human well-being. In view of the value of religion to its adherants, the Humanist movement makes no attempt to convert religious people to Humanism. The Humanist message is directed to people who have lost their faith or who have never had one.

THE PROBLEM OF EVIL

Question Fifteen
What is the Humanist attitude to the problem of evil?

For the Humanist, the theological problem of evil does not exist. The problem is: how can we reconcile the existence of undeserved pain, disease, disaster and misery with a loving and all-powerful heavenly Father? The existence of a good and all-powerful God is not logically compatible with a world in which there is widespread evil. If God is all-powerful and allows so much evil to exist He cannot be loving and if He is loving in the present of evil he cannot be all-powerful. There have been many attempts to solve this problem, one of the most commonly quoted being that we should have faith in God whose ways are beyond human understanding. But theologians admit that there is no completely satisfactory answer.

The problem does not exist for Humanists because they do not accept the idea of a loving all-powerful God, or any god, to account for the existence of the universe. The many events and influences in the world that reduce the welfare and happiness of mankind do not therefore present a special philosophical problem to Humanists: they regard them simply as part of existence. The problem for Humanists is: What actions should be taken to remove or alleviate those things that are regarded as evil?

The Humanist answer is that modern science and technology can do a great deal to avoid natural disasters, or reduce their effects. Floods can be prevented by increasing drainage, the effect of droughts can be prevented by building dams and by irrigation. Earthquakes and volcanoes can, in some cases, now be predicted so that warnings can be issued and emergency services alerted, as is also possible with severe weather conditions such as hurricanes or blizzards. The movement of epidemics over continents is predictable so that medicines to prevent and cure them can be prepared in advance. Thus, the impact of many events that were major disasters in the past is now being reduced.

One of the greatest developments of the 20th century has been the rapid rise in the study of social sciences, which it is hoped will eventually bring within our grasp the control of many man-made evils such as war, poverty, crime, accidents and pollution. The signs are that humankind is beginning to learn that its prosperity, and possibly its survival, depends on more international co-operation. The existence of the United Nations, provides a machinery, if still very imperfect, for dealing with international disputes. Modern knowledge of economics suggests that we have the means to achieve prosperity and avoid the extremes of rich and poor not only within nations but also between nations. Unfortunately, the political will to apply this knowledge is still lacking.

Humanists, by freeing their minds from the theological approach to evil, are better able to concentrate their energy on how to deal with natural and man-made evils.

The Christian and Humanist Views on the Nature of Humankind
The Christian view of humankind is that it is a fallen species of miserable sinners who can achieve nothing on its own but must constantly seek God's help. To the Humanist, this view is as psychologically damaging as it is lacking in evidence. Living things have, for over 3000 million years, obtained their food and shelter, reproduced their kind and evolved into fitter species but until the arrival of civilised humanity, neither one syllable of petitionary prayer nor a single paean of praise were offered to God. Why therefore is it thought that humankind, the most able of all species, cannot survive or develop without God's help? Although, of course, fully realising that some people behave in an antisocial manner, Humanists regard the human race as a magnificent species capable of immense feats of creativeness, invention, organisation and benevolence and unique in that it can exert some control over its evolution and destiny. Civilised humanity is still in its infancy compared with many other

species, some of which have existed for millions of years. Serious study and action to alleviate disease, misery and poverty on an international scale are very recent developments, measured only in decades. Humanists do not claim the power of prophecy, but in spite of severe set-backs at the time of writing (November 1992) there has been a steady improvement in the human lot in many parts of the world during the present century. The increased concern for human suffering gives ground for hope that the challenge of evil will be met effectively in the immense future that probably lies ahead of the human race.

FREE WILL AND DETERMINISM

Question Sixteen
What is the Humanist attitude to free will and determinism?

Free will (or libertarianism) is the belief that people have liberty to choose the way they behave. Determinism, on the other hand, implies that people have no freedom of choice and that their actions are determined by the influence of their genes and of their environment over which they have no control.

In Europe, this debate came into prominence with the introduction of Christianity. The Christians thought in terms of an all-powerful God that controlled the universe and everything in it. This meant that man was controlled by God and therefore had no personal choice about his thoughts and behaviour. St Augustine (354-430) was the first Christian writer to realise that this led to a problem. He thought that mankind had free will but also believed in an all-powerful God. He failed to solve the problem: if man is free, how can God be all-powerful?

The issue of free will versus determinism does not arise until we consider the state of organisation of matter/energy in the human body and perhaps the higher animals. In the realm of non-living matter and of most living things, determinism is generally held to obtain. (The quantum theory postulates that the behaviour of electrons is not determined but this is not relevant in any practical way to objects in everyday life). Human beings, with their development of thought and imagination, think that they have the ability to choose between several courses of action. But is this impression that we are free to choose what we do, an illusion? It is obvious that some circumstances of our lives are determined by our heredity and environment. For example, anyone born in a remote Third World village will have a very different behaviour pattern and outlook on life compared with someone born in a prosperous European town. The question is whether all our decisions and conduct are completely determined by our genes and past experience.

The argument between free will and determinism still goes on after many centuries and the thinking on both sides is subtle. It is a philosophical and not a scientific question in that it depends on argument and speculation and cannot be tested by any obvious experiment. There is no space here to analyse the problem and to summarise the lengthy and complicated arguments but it can be said that neither side has won and this problem may never be solved. Although some Humanists may favour the determinist position philosophically, in everyday life they accept that adults have free will and legally they are expected to bear the full responsibility for what they do and how they behave. The courts now accept 'diminished responsibility' or 'extenuating circumstances' as a defence i.e. they accept that the behaviour of some people has been determined by genetic and environmental influences and that they lack the free will that normal people are assumed to have. The courts may offer treatment that attempts rehabilitation in the belief that free will and normal behaviour can be restored.

If determinists are correct, they do not arrive at their conclusion after carefully weighing up the arguments, but are led to one conclusion, because, on their own admission, they are compelled to reach that conclusion by their genetic make-up and their previous experiences. Also, if determinists are right, we are mere puppets and any discussion of moral principles is simply a charade controlled by our determined lines of thought. Whilst this possibility cannot be denied, and we have no rational means of deciding the issue, Humanists accept in practice our clear impression that we have an element of free will and can exert some decisive influence over our actions.

Some religious teaching has taken the line that everything that happens has been in the mind of God since the beginning of time and that it cannot be changed. This can lead to the idea that there is no point in making any effort to change our living conditions because the future is fixed. The effect of this is to induce people to be fatalistic and to submit to poverty, squalor and disease instead of working to master and improve conditions so as to raise the quality of human life. Humanists emphatically reject this line of thinking.

THE MEANING AND PURPOSE OF LIFE

Question Seventeen
What do Humanists think are the meaning and purpose of life? Why does the world exist?

Humanists realise that they cannot discern any meaning or purpose in the universe, the existence of which they regard as an inexplicable mystery and they are prepared to live with this. In the pre-scientific age it was taken for granted that the universe was created by God for the benefit of humanity but science has shown that, on the scale of the universe as a whole, man is utterly insignificant in both space and time. People who believe in a divine creator may think that the creator had some purpose in mind but what that purpose was is not clear. The short answer is, therefore, that Humanists cannot see any long-term meaning or purpose in the universe but this does not depress them.

Scientists predict that there will come a time, thousands of millions of years hence when all life on earth will cease as the sun expands into a red giant star and overheats, or even engulfs, the earth. On the astronomical time scale, it could be argued that life has no purpose because of its eventual extinction. However, we are not concerned with such a time scale in everyday life and if we consider the present and immediate future of individuals they can, to a large extent, choose their own purpose in life. Some may consider their careers as their main activity, others may give priority to raising a family while yet others may give their main energies into hobbies and sports. In other words, life can have a very real purpose, or combine several purposes in each individual.

Humankind is Still a Youthful Species
Although the human species separated from its ape-like ancestors several millions of years ago, humankind has known civilisation for less than 10,000 years and what might be called modern technological humanity is a very youthful type indeed,

being scarcely a century old. Humanity may reasonably expect to survive for millions of years although, during this time, there may be need to cope with some serious set-backs, such as the spread of AIDS and the long-term effects of environmental pollution on human health. The total effect of improvements in the human environment from discoveries, inventions and more equitable political and social structures introduced now or in the near future could be enormous when measured in terms of the permanent benefit to countless future generations. Surely this thought provides a most challenging incentive for action and a most worthwhile purpose in life!

Is there a design and purpose in evolution?
Some have argued that the process of evolution reveals a design and purpose in living things such as the purpose of becoming ever fitter to survive and to enjoy the world's resources. If there is evidence of design, it is argued that God was the designer. However, although evolution has shown a tendency towards increased complexity and fitness this has not always been so. Many species have become extinct without leaving any successors, others have undergone a change towards earlier forms e.g. birds that have lost the ability to fly, and mammals that have returned to the sea (whence early life came) to evolve into whales and seals. Also, in spite of the almost incredible efficiency of living things, too many features look like errors of design to suggest an intelligent creator. The Russian biologist Metchnikoff listed one hundred and twenty 'design faults' in the human body that might have been avoided if it had been designed by an engineer. One example is the complications, without any obvious advantages, arising from the fact that in the higher animals the millions of nerve fibres leaving each side of the brain cross over to control the opposite side of the body. Furthermore, it would not seem that a good designer, much less a loving one, would ever arrange that so many species of animals can survive only by the merciless killing and eating of other species. The existence of herbivorous animals and vegetarian human beings shows that flesh-eating is not a necessity for life. See also page 33.

Why does the world exist?

This is a reasonable question to ask by anyone who believes in a God who created the world, as presumably He must have had some purpose in mind when He created it. The traditional view, based on the idea that the earth was the centre of the universe, has been that God created it to provide a home for humankind. But this leaves unanswered the question: Why did He do this? As Humanists reject the idea of a Creator and it is common knowledge that, far from being the centre of the universe, the earth is an insignificant speck in the unimaginably vast universe, this idea about the purpose of the world is unacceptable. The only frank answer that the Humanist can given is that there is no information on which to base a conjecture as to why the world or the universe exists.

DEATH AND LIFE AFTER DEATH

Question Eighteen
Do Humanists believe in life after death?

The short answer is 'no'. And it may be added neither do they believe in life before birth - the idea that individual personalities have lived before (reincarnation). However, this short answer needs some qualification.

To maintain life, the organism must take in food and oxygen for body building and the provision of energy. This internal chemical activity is called metabolism and while the organism is alive its metabolism maintains a balance between the intake of food, water and oxygen for growth and the output of energy and waste. In human beings, when the oxygen supply to the brain stops for more than a few minutes the brain cells begin to deteriorate and soon cease to control the body. When the control finally ends it is impossible to restart it and the body is dead. After death, the body soon begins to decompose into less complex compounds which eventually become available to plants and other animals thus completing the cycle of life. What remains? The Humanist finds it difficult to believe that anything remains. There is no scientific evidence for the existence of a soul and it is difficult to believe that the mind can exist independently of the body.

However, in two respects a person does live on after death. In the first place, sexual reproduction means that some of the characteristics of parents are passed on through their genes to their offspring and to future generations. Secondly, with the development of speech, writing, drawing and with other modern methods of recording, many people have had and will continue to have great influence after their deaths. Dawkins has coined the word 'memes' (from 'memory' and 'genes') to indicate that new ideas by spreading from brain to brain can replicate (like genes) and have an ever-widening influence through present and future generations.

The following important conclusions result from the Humanist attitude to death:

1) The Humanist does not expect a future life of bliss in a heaven.
2) The Humanist concentrates on aiming to improve the quality of life on earth - the only life we are sure about.

Reincarnation

In recent years there has been a renewed interest in reincarnation, the idea that after the death of one person the 'soul' returns to life in a new-born baby. There are reports of people, sometimes under hypnosis, claiming to have recollections of events in a former existence – although it is possible that these people have read or heard about these events and forgotten them and later recalled them from their subconscious. Humanists do not consider this evidence to be a serious challenge to their disbelief in the after-life. A further argument against belief in reincarnation is that, as the population of the world is increasing, the number of babies being born is larger than the number of people dying. In other words, if reincarnation does occur, there would be too few 'souls' available to enter bodies of new-born babies!

Humanist Funeral Ceremonies

As Humanists do not believe that we survive after death, it naturally follows that they do not think that prayers and funeral ceremonies have any effect on the dead. Funerals are for the benefit of the living and have a role in relieving tension, coming to terms with grief and providing an opportunity for paying a tribute to the deceased and offering consolation to relatives and friends.

Humanists realise that the conventional Christian funeral is completely inappropriate for those who do not believe in the after-life. Whenever possible, a bereaved Humanist family arranges a non-religious funeral ceremony (it should not, perhaps, be called a service). Such a ceremony can typically include a brief summary of the deceased's life and achievements with special reference to his contributions to Humanist ideals. In addition, there would be words of comfort (sometimes consisting of poems or quotations from well-known sources) to friends and relatives. The British Humanist Association (address and telephone number on page 3) has organised a list of people willing to conduct secular funerals (and marriages and naming ceremonies). Requests are welcomed but it is not always possible to provide these ceremonies in all parts of the country. The BHA has also published a useful booklet ('Funerals without God' price £3) which includes suggested formats for secular funerals along with poems and quotations suitable for inclusion. Many Humanists would like to see the formal establishment of secular funerals in much the same way as in Britain there are civil marriages.

The Biological Significance of Death
Death has important biological and sociological consequences. If people continued to be born and never died the world would rapidly become over-populated. Also, evolution depends on the death and replacement of successive generations. Today the world's population is rising, because improvements in the environment and in medical services reduce infantile mortality and allow adults to live longer and have more children (See Question 19).

Parasychology and the Question of Survival
Parapsychology (also known as psychic research) attempts to study by modern methods various phenomena, real or supposed, that have not yet been explained some of which are relevant to the question of survival after death.

Over the centuries, many people have reported going through an experience described as 'seeing a ghost' especially in some building or location reputed to be 'haunted'. Although the occurrence of these experiences cannot be denied, their cause or causes are highly controversial. In many cases, they may arise from optical illusions, hallucinations or other natural events. When under emotional stress, some people have difficulty in separating reality from fantasy. Scientific studies have not led to any conclusion about the nature of these experiences but they provide no evidence for the popular explanation that 'ghosts' are the spirits of dead people.

Spiritualism is a religious movement whose adherents believe in the afterlife and that specially sensitive people (mediums) can communicate with the dead. Some of these claims (but not all) have been exposed as frauds and many 'messages' are so vague as to have no evidential value. Again, scientific investigations have failed to establish either the validity of the messages or their source. One approach to the question of survival attempted by a few scientists has been to leave a sealed or coded message with the object of challenging mediums to see whether they can receive the message or crack the code after the experimenter had died. There are no reports of a successful outcome.

Death-bed experiences
The reported experiences of dying people, and especially those who, with modern medical technology, have been resuscitated after short periods of apparent death, have shown remarkable similarities. One group of reports mention an 'out of body experience' in which the individuals appear to have floated above their bodies and were able to see and hear doctors and nurses trying to revive them and, in some, cases, pronouncing them to be dead. Other experiences are of passing along a dark passage with lights at the end, of seeing relatives who were already dead and of a feeling of intense peace and serenity (so much so that a few patients were quite resentful that they had been resuscitated!). Although these experiences have been quoted as evidence for the entry of the dying into another world it is well-established that one effect of lack of oxygen (which occurs with failing circulation as death approaches) is hallucination and a feeling of elation. Lack of oxygen might therefore explain these experiences.

Scientific Attitudes towards Parapsychology
Many people, including some scientists and Humanists (but how many is not known, because we are not aware of any opinion polls having been carried out on this question) dismiss the whole subject of parapsychology as 'impossible' because it

seems to contradict their whole pattern of thought. On the other hand, some scientists welcome the study of this subject on the grounds that they wish to keep their minds open and be constantly on the look-out for new knowledge. They argue that if any of the claims of parapsychology prove to be true they would have a great influence on scientific and philosophical thought and in might even be possible to use them to increase human welfare.

POPULATION GROWTH AND WORLD RESOURCES

Question Nineteen
How can human welfare be improved in view of the rapid growth of the world's population?

The UN estimated figures for world populations are:

Year	Population (millions)	Percentage of population based on 1800
1800	840	100
1900	1550	184
2000	6100	729
2025	8200	973

The above table shows the acceleration in the estimated rate of population increase – in the 25 years from 2000 to 2025 it is over 30% (2100 millions) – more than the entire world population in 1900 (1550 millions). This accelerating growth raises the spectre of the demand for world resources outstripping the supply, resulting in greater poverty especially in the Third World comprising Asia, Africa, Central and South America. This rapid rise in population has occurred from:

1) A sharp reduction in infantile mortality so that more babies than previously survive to maturity.
2) A fall in the adult death rate has also occurred in many countries so that more adults now enjoy a longer life. The percentage of people over 60 is rapidly increasing especially in developed countries.

Thus the world could be faced with shortages of food, energy and many of the consumer goods that we have come to expect as being necessary for a higher standard of living. This could make it not only more difficult to raise living standards in developing countries but also more difficult to maintain existing standards in developed countries. In addition, there is the problem of environmental pollution arising from the increasing volumes of waste products.

There are three main ways in which this serious problem may be tackled.

1)   Checking the rise in population growth

In westernised countries, the rate of population growth has decreased greatly over the last century, during which time the standard of living has increased. The probable reason for this is that in developing countries (as European countries were in the last century) a large family can be an economic asset, costing little to educate but providing a free labour force for producing the family's food or helping with a family business. It also provides a miniature built-in welfare state as some members of the family can act as child minders and others care for the elderly. In highly developed countries, however, bringing up and educating children is very expensive and few parents can expect their children to contribute regularly to the family income or look after them in old age. Many women, too, rebel against the tedium and hard work involved in excessive child bearing. It is a matter of speculation as to whether the reduction in family size that occurred in westernised countries will occur in the Third World as its economy develops. Also, it cannot be assumed that the prosperity of the developing countries will expand sufficiently quickly to produce the conditions associated with reduced birth rates before population reaches an unmanageable size.

Humanists think, therefore, that international efforts should be made to press governments of countries with a high birth-rate to encourage family planning. There are difficulties arising from religious doctrines, from unwillingness to change old customs or modes of thought; many people resent being told what to do on such a personal matter as family size. Nevertheless, some countries have enforced family limitation and have met these difficulties. For example, China in 1979 introduced a policy of only one child per family. The aim was to stabilize the population at 1.2 billion by the year 2000. Although this policy did have a welcome effect in reducing population growth, by 1988 China had to admit that the policy could no longer be enforced. Peasants wanted boys (some even killed girl babies) and were allowed to have a second child if the first was a girl. Other families had to pay a fine if they had a second child. The estimated future population was raised to 1.25 billion by 2000 with stabilization hoped for by 2050. India has had similar difficulties with attempts to introduce male sterilization.

2)   Making better use of existing resources.

There are many ways of achieving this of which the following are the most important:

a)   Only about 20% of the earth's land surface is at present used for food production. It is vitally important to maintain this area and to prevent its reduction by soil erosion. This can be done by contour ploughing, by preserving existing forests and by replacing trees that have been felled and by returning humus (i.e. organic matter) to the soil.

b)   Much food is lost by attack from insects, moulds, bacteria and rodents. This could be prevented or reduced by improved methods of storage.

c)   Much energy is wasted by inefficiency, e.g. badly insulated houses, engines with a high fuel consumption and failure to utilise waste heat from industrial processes.

3)   Production of food and energy by new or improved methods.

There are many ways of doing this of which the following are some typical examples:

a)   Among methods for increasing food production are the following: increasing the area of land used for agriculture e.g. by irrigating deserts and draining swamps; producing, by selective breeding and genetic engineering, strains of plants and animals with higher yields of food; greater use of fertilisers (with care to avoid pollution of rivers); use of the quick growing foods, such as yeast, as sources of protein and vitamins; intensive production of plant food in greenhouses and animal foods in batteries (with care to minimize cruelty to animals); encouragement of vegetable foods in preference to animal products (which, although more nutritious, are very wasteful to produce); expansion of fishing in tropical seas and of fish farming.

b)   Energy

Research is now in progress (though not on as large a scale as might be hoped) on the generation of electricity from solar energy, the energy of wind, waves, tides and heat from the earth's interior. Nuclear energy from fission (the release of energy by the break up (fission) of uranium atoms by bombarding them with neutrons) is already in use but suffers from the disadvantage that it leads to the accumulation of radio-active end-products whose long term storage presents a problem. This is avoided in the alternative form of nuclear energy – nuclear fusion (hydrogen atoms are fused together to form helium with the release of an enormous quantity of energy, see page 21) but the harnessing of this energy on a practical scale has not yet been perfected.

Thus, by a mixture of using scientific knowledge to provide more resources and by the still controversial method of population control (strongly supported by Humanists) the world may be able to cope with a much larger population. All this will, of course, require an increase in the most important resource of all – human skill and knowledge. This will make possible a much greater application of technology based on scientific method – the very essence of Humanism.

CONCLUSION

Question Twenty
Humanism may be acceptable and satisfying to the learned scientist but does it meet everybody's needs?

It is true that Humanist ideas were originated by highly educated people as they were the first to see the difficulties of religious belief and were sufficiently independent to express their views without fear of the consequences. However, today many people with only a rudimentary knowledge of science find that religious beliefs strain their credulity. The decline of church-going in most parts of the western world suggests that many people can and do live their daily lives without any religious practices. On the other hand some people who find it difficult to accept religious belief feel they have no 'anchor' in life nor any basis for morals. Individuals who have been brought up with a religious faith which has gradually faded, may need some mental readjustment to face up to the Humanist belief that the human race is alone and that there is no supernatural force that can be turned to for help.

The Humanist position is really very simple and can be understood by anyone. It emphasises that the here and now of this life is all that we can be sure of and we should make the most of it. Humanist moral values, beginning with the surely indisputable belief that human well-being is to be preferred to human misery, provide a simple basis for the good life. Actions that raise the level of human well-being are right and good; those with the reverse effect are to be avoided or discouraged. The practical application of this can lead to a whole range of activities from being friendly and helpful to a lonely neighbour to supporting and working for the various organisations concerned with raising living and health standards throughouts the world.

Thus Humanism can give a sense of purpose and provide a background for a satisfying and exhilarating life for everybody.

INDEX